DearScott

Dear Scott

Compiled by Scott Deindorfer

Workman Publishing, New York

Library of Congress Cataloging in Publication Data
Main entry under title:
Dear Scott.
    Summary: A compilation of favorite quotations and
sayings of more than 200 well-known Americans.
    1. Quotations, English. [1. Quotations]
I. Deindorfer, Scott.
PN6081.D45 081 77-5304
ISBN 0-89480-007-8

Workman Publishing Company
1 West 39 Street
New York, New York 10018

Manufactured in the United States of America

First printing May 1978

10   9   8   7   6   5   4   3   2   1

I compiled this book because I'm interested in famous people in different fields and have often wondered whether they have had a particular quotaion or saying that helped them rise to the top.

I am surprised at and thankful for the number of personal responses I received from extremely busy people, which hust prove that these favorite quotations are important to them. If this is so, they might be important to you, too.

Part of the earnings from this book will be contributed to the American Cancer Society, the American Heart Association, and the Save the Children Fund. I have chosen these organizations because they seem to me especially worthy.

If anyone ever asked me for my favorite saying there would be so many that it would be difficult to decide, but I have managed to narrow the choice down to two. One is "Time is a river without banks," and the other is "Do unto others as you would have them do unto you."

Scott Deindorfer

New York
May 1978

Conrad Hilton

Inspire us with wisdom, all of us of every color, race and creed,
to use our wealth, our strength to help our brother, instead of destroying him.

from "The Battle for Peace,"
an address by Conrad N. Hilton

Conrad M Hilton

Isaac Asimov

"The difference between the right word and the nearly
right word is the difference between the lightning
and the lightning-bug".

That's a good thing for a writer to remember.

Isaac Asimov

Victor Borge

"A SMILE IS THE SHORTEST

DISTANCE BETWEEN TWO PEOPLE".

John Wayne

When the road looks rough ahead, remember
the "Man Upstairs" and the word H-O-P-E.
Hang onto both and tough it out."

Cornelia Otis Skinner

"THIS DAY WE SAILED ON"
Christopher Columbus

Cornelia Otis Skinner

Ricky Bell

"When the going gets tough,
the tough get going."

Author unknown

John Knowles, M.D.

"Humor is the prelude to faith,
and laughter the beginning of prayer."

Paul Tillich

John H. Knowles, M.D.

Jody Powell

When we pray, we should
ask for mercy, not justice.

Paul Moore

"It is the cracked ones that
let the light through."

Mary Tyler Moore

"If it doesn't hurt, you're not doing it right"

Mary Tyler Moore

Julian Bond

"Study long, but
don't study wrong."

Julian Bond

Murray the K

" If you can't do it right, don't do it
at all... But darn it - you should wal
on it till you get it right-

Murray the K

Gene Wilder

"Be very careful of what you want—
because you might get it."

Gene Wilder

Dan Greenburg

"Better know what you want,
because you'll probably
get it."

Dan Greenburg

Henry Winkler

My key to life is knowing what you
want . Once knowing that it is
no longer a dream.

Harvey G. Cox

"Consistency is the hobgoblin of little minds.'

Ralph Waldo Emerson

Walter Mondale

You can make mistakes around here

but you can't lie.

His Father

Liza Minelli

Don't complain.
Don't explain.

Ella Grasso

My two favorite sayings are "Pacienza - patience" and "Don't think, ask."

Ella Grasso

Johnny Cash

"IF IT WAS EASY,

ANYBODY COULD DO IT."

William M. Batten

In three ways man can achieve knowledge:
the way of thinking - the noble way;
the way of trial and error - the hard way;
and the way of imitation - the easy way.

Confucius

W. M. Batten

Heywood Hale Broun

ambition often puts men upon doing the meanest offices
So, climbing is performed in the same posture with
creeping

Heywood Hale Broun

Jonathan Swift

George McGovern

"What doth the Lord require of thee,
but to do justly, and to love mercy,
and to walk humbly with thy God?"

Micah 6:8

Elliot L. Richardson

"How you stand depends
on where you sit."

Miles's Law

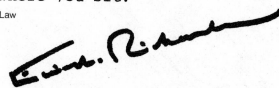

Rusty Staub

The most important person for anyone to learn about, know, understand and believe in other than God is himself. Conquering yourself is one of the most important things any person can do. For then you qualify to help others.

To Truly

Carol Burnett

My favorite is a definition of luck. First said by the late Ed Wynn: "Luck is when opportunity meets with preparation." I have always believed that we are all given opportunities in life, but many of us just aren't properly prepared when they come. Then so many people say that they are 'unlucky.' I just don't believe that.

Carol Burnett

Jerry Stiller

"That which does not kill me only makes me stronger ..

Jeremiah Morris

Jerry Stiller

Roger Staubach

"I can do all things
through Christ who
strengtheneth me."

Roger Staubach

Helen Hayes

"Patience, and
shuffle the cards."

Larry Csonka

"All men are created equal ... except the great ones!"

Larry Csonka '77

Margaret "Midge" Costanza

"I am not a woman who just happens to be an Assistant to The President. I am an Assistant to The President who just happens to be a woman."

Tom Bradley

"Some men see things as they are and say: why?
I dream things that never were and say: why not?"

George Bernard Shaw

Tom Bradley

Henny Youngman

Take my wife, please

Henny Youngman

Bob Hope

"Laugh and the world
laughs with you, cry
and you drive a comedian
to the nut house."

Bob Hope

Earl Wilson

Never give advice

(Sell it!)"

Earl Wilson

Eunice Kennedy Shriver

"Let me win, but if I cannot win,
let me be brave in the attempt"

Oath of mentally retarded competitors
in the Special Olympics

Eunice K. Shriver

Don F. Shula

SUCCESS ISN'T FINAL --
FAILURE ISN'T FATAL

Author Unknown

Don F Shula

Paul Samuelson

" Truth cannot be told so as to be understood
without being believed."

William Blake

Paul Samuelson

Ronald Reagan

"You can accomplish much if you don't care who gets the credit."

Ronald Reagan

Anonymous

Audrey Meadows

One of my favorite sayings is a quote from a coach I worked with for many years in New York. His name is Bert Knapp and he has coached people like Gig Young, Ben Gazzara, Peter Falk, etc., etc, and his quote is, "You as you are are better by far than the you that you are trying to be".

Audrey Meadows

Hugh Downs

"The downfall of a magician is belief in his own magic." Author unknown

Bill Bradley

```
Of a good leader
When his work is done
    his aim fulfilled
The people will say,
'We did this ourselves.'
```

Bill Bradley

Madeline Kahn

"you in your way, me in mine."

Madeline Kahn

Norman Vincent Peale

"Silence is the element in which great

things fashion themselves."

Thomas Carlyle

Norman Vincent Peale

Lowell Thomas

Knowledge puffeth up, but charity edifieth. And if any man thinks that he knoweth anything, he knows nothing yet as he ought to know.

First Corinthians 8:1-2

Harriet Van Horne

"The simple believeth every word, but the prudent man looketh well to his going."

Book of Proverbs

Sam J. Ervin, Jr.

"We should let nothing on this side of the grave put an end to our search for knowledge."

Henry Cabot Lodge

"to strive, to seek, to find, and not to yield"

Alfred Tennyson

Pierre Trudeau

Man has reached out and touched the tranquil moon. May this high endeavor inspire mankind to re-discover the earth and find peace there.

from the Prime Minister's message on Apollo XI's moon landing

G. Keith Funston

"Ad astra per aspera."

To the stars through hardships.

Henry Miller

" Don't look for miracles "
You are the miracle. "   *Henry Miller*

Mrs. Leonard Lyons

Nobody's ever insulted
to be invited.

Mrs. Leonard Lyons

Jimmy Carter

Behold, I stand at the door and knock; if any one hears my voice

and opens the door, I will come in to him and eat with him, and he

with me.

Revelations 3:15

Jimmy Carter

Gene Tunney

"A friend may well be reckoned
the masterpiece of nature."

Ralph Waldo Emerson

Walter Cronkite

"Post proof that brotherhood is
one and not so wild a dream as
those who would profit by posting
it pretned."

Norman Corwin

Ann Landers

"The true measure of a man is how he treats
someone who can do him absolutely no good."

Mamie Eisenhower

A self made man and proud of his maker —
Mamie Eisenhower

Sister Mary Luke Tobin

"I have just a few years in which to do my work, which I love, so I must be serious about it."

Sister Luke Tobin.

Nureyev

Andrew Young

"They shall beat their swords into
plowshares, and their spears into
pruning hooks; nations shall not
lift sword against nation, neither
shall they learn war any more."

Isaiah 2:4

Admiral E. R. Zumwalt, Jr.

"Damn the torpedoes!
- Full speed ahead!"

Farragut

Sam Brown

Pray for the
dead, fight like hell
for the living.

Mother Jones

Irving Wallace

"I believe that it is better to tell the truth than a
lie. I believe it is better to be free than a slave. And
I believe it is better to know than to be ignorant."

H. L. Mencken

Meadowlark Lemon

"Deal in nothing less than the truth.
Never cheat a friend.
Always, always deal in truth."

MEADOWLARK LEMON

Vincent Sardi, Jr.

DON'T WORRY.
LIFE'S TOO <u>LONG.</u>

[signature: Vincent Sardi]

Frank Gifford

"Most of the things you worry about don't happen...
and when they do, most of the time they weren't
worth worrying about".

This statement made an impression on me the first
time I heard it and have never forgotten that it
came from the late T. J. Mara founder of the
New York Giants and the man who gave me my 1st
pro football contract.

[signature: Frank Gifford]

Clifford Irving

"What you're worrying about won't happen, but something
else will." It's original.

[signature: Clifford Irving]

Naomi Sims

" Let us think only of spending the present
day well. Then when tomorrow shall have
come, it will be called today, and then
we will think about it."
St. Francis de Sales

Naomi Sims

Father Theodore Hesburgh

"All I know of tomorrow is that providence
will rise before the dawn."
Pere Lacordaire

Alvin Toffler

"Remember
the
Future!"

Mary McGrory &
Gerald R. Ford

"Count where man's glory
Most begins and ends
And say, my glory was
I had such friends."

William Butler Yeats

Jerry Ford

Mary McGrory

Sugar Ray Robinson

"I am a God fearing man and it is my daily prayer if I be lifted up, I will draw all men unto me."

Sugar Ray Robinson

Shana Alexander

"Lash the vice, but spare the name."

Jonathan Swift

Shana Alexander

Beverly Sills

" If you can't say something nice about someone, don't say anything at all"

B. Kliban

[illegible]

B Kliban

James Cagney

Your family name is an interesting one. "Dein" means "to serve" and "Dorfer" is "town."

J Cagney

Jeane Dixon

"If we triumph in the little things of our
common hours, we are sure to triumph in our
lives...and we will find that work is love
in action -- hence His Will, will be done."

Edward M. Kennedy

When we were young children, my father
always impressed us with his wish that we
would commit our lives in some way to serving
others. Therefore, one of my favorite quotations comes from the Bible -- Luke 12, 48

For unto whomsoever much is given,
of him shall be much required;
And to whom men have committed much,
of him they will ask the more.

James Robinson

"Do something. Lead, follow,
or get out of the way."

Mark O. Hatfield

"...Words without actions are the
assassins of idealism."
Herbert Hoover

Billie Jean King

Never confuse movement
with action.

David J. Mahoney

"Trust movement-see what happens not what you
feel should or would happen in a situation, life
happens at the level of events, not of words."

Helen Yglesias

" Show me a gracious loser and I'll
show you a loser. "

Helen Yglesias

Art Linkletter &
Bert Lance

SUCCESS IS A JOURNEY
AND NOT A DESTINATION.

Bert Lance

Bear Bryant

" Winning Isn't Everything
But It Beats Whatever Is Second. "

John Toland

"If once you don't succeed, try, try again."
That has been the story of my life. I started writing when I was 14
years old but my first story was not published until I was 42.

Good luck

O.J. Simpson

"Once one has tasted the
success of being the very
best, it's hard to
settle for anything less."

Arnold Palmer

Life's battles always don't go

To the stronger or faster man.

But sooner or later the man who wins

Is the fellow who thinks he can.

General William C. Westmoreland & Frank Borman

Nothing in the world can take the place of persistence. Talent will not; nothing is more common than unsuccessful men with talent. Genius will not; unrewarded genius is almost a proverb. Education alone will not; the world is full of educated derelicts. Persistence and determination alone are omnipotent.

Calvin Coolidge

[signature]

[signature]

Mitch Miller & Col. Harlan Sanders

A MAN WILL RUST OUT

QUICKER THAN HE WILL

WEAR OUT.

Joan Ganz Cooney

" *Teach us to care and not to care* " —

T. S. Eliot

Joan Ganz Cooney

Jerry Lewis

"I shall pass through this world but once and good, therefore, that I can do or any kindness that I can show to any human being, let me do it now.

Let me not deter nor neglect it, for I shall not pass this way again.

Etiénne Grellet

Jerry Lewis

John Cheever

"Let us consider that the soul of man is immortal, able to endure every sort of good and every sort of evil. Thus may we live happily with one another and with the Gods."

John Cheever

Marshall McLuhan

Apropos my saying "the medium is the message", it is a way of drawing attention to the hidden <u>ground</u> that accompanies all noticeable <u>figures</u>. That is why the program content on any medium, whether radio or TV or print or telephone, has a very small effect in shaping the lives of people, compared to the medium itself.

E.g.

The motor car is a <u>figure</u> in a huge <u>ground</u> of services which includes highways, manufactures, and gas and oil services. This vast <u>ground</u> of services affects everybody all the time, whether anybody is driving a car or not. It is this huge <u>ground</u> that is the "message" of the car.

Good wishes

Marshall McLuhan

Archie Manning

"A man's true wealth is the good he does in this world."

Bendixline

Gloria Vanderbilt

```
Much that I sought I could not find;

Much that I found I could not bind;

Much that I bound I could not free;

Much that I freed returned to me.
```

Lee Wilson Dodd

Andrew Heiskell

"If a man does not keep pace with his
companions, perhaps it is because he
hears a different drummer. Let him
step to the music which he hears, however
measured or far away."

Henry David Thoreau

Andrew Heiskell

Debbie Boone

"The Lord is my strength & my shield;
my heart trusts in Him & I am helped;
Therefore my heart exults,
And with my song I shall thank Him."

Psalm 28: 7-10

Dean Rusk & Willis Reed

"Let him who is without
sin **cast** the first stone."

John 8:7

Dean Rusk

Monte Irvin

"OUT OF EVERY BAD SITUATION
CAN DEVELOP SOME GOOD."

George C. Wallace

"As you have done it unto one of the least of
these my brethren, you have done it
also unto me."

Matthew 25:40

George C Wallace

Alan Funt

" IT'S ALWAYS EARLY FOR SOMETHING "

Alan Funt

Helen Gurley Brown

" The best time is <u>now</u>. "

Helen

Milton Caniff

" Everything comes to him who waits — and in waiting, works. "

Milton Caniff

James L. Isham , Phyllis Diller & John B. Connally

"This above all: to thine own
self be true,
And it must follow, as the
 night the day,
Thou canst not then be false
 to any man."

Shakespeare

James L. Isham

John Connally

Phyllis Diller

Henry Luce III & Birch Bayh

"Give me the serenity to accept
what cannot be changed;
"Give me the courage to change
what must be changed;
"The wisdom to distinguish
one from the other."

Birch Bayh

Henry Luce III

Angelo Bertelli

Life is a matter
of timing.

Joan Sutherland

"Nothing can bring you
peace but yourself."

Ralph Waldo Emerson

Eileen Ford

My favorite quote is " Thank you."
Haven't heard it in years.

Wilbur Mills

"live & let live"

[signature: W.D. Mills]

Ralph Martin

" milk it ! "

Jan Morris

You never can tell!

[signature: Jan Morris]

Lawrence Welk

"Wunnerful! Wunnerful!"

[signature: Lawrence Welk]

Betty Ford

PRAYER OF
ST. FRANCIS OF ASSISI

Lord, make me an instrument
  of your peace.

Where there is hatred, let me
  sow love;

where there is injury, pardon;
  where there is doubt, faith;

where there is despair, hope;
where there is darkness, light;

and where there is sadness, joy.

O Divine Master, grant that
  I may not so much seek to be

consoled as to console; to be
  understood as to understand;

to be loved as to love; for it is
  in giving that we receive;

it is in pardoning that we are
  pardoned;

and it is in dying that we are
  born to eternal life.

Nelson A. Rockefeller

"Though I speak with the tongues of
men and of angels, and have not love,
I am become as sounding brass, or a
tinkling cymbal...And now abideth faith,
hope, love, these three; but the greatest
of these is love."

First Corinthians 13: 1-3

Zsa Zsa Gabor

"LOVE IS WEAKNESS,
TO BE LOVED IS STRENGTH."

French Proverb

Alta

"It is when we cease to love one another, when we

cease to hold one another, that the sea engulfs us

and the light goes out."

James Baldwin

Fitzhugh Dodson

"Most men win only victories;

the rare man wins defeat."

Bonaro Overstreet

James M. Gavin

"Without vision the

people shall perish."

Book of Proverbs

Billy Graham

Thou wilt show me the path of life:
In thy presence is fullness of joy;
at thy right hand there are
pleasures for evermore.

Psalm 16:11

Bernard Berkowitz

IF I am not for myself – then who can be for me, and
IF I'm only for myself – what am I, and
IF not now, when?

Hillel

Roy Scheider

"We have met the enemy and they are us."

Walt Kelly's "Pogo"

Roy Scheider

Glen Campbell

My dad always said, "Treat other people as you like to be treated", and that's now my favorite saying.

Glen Campbell

Edwin E. "Buzz" Aldrin, Jr.

No DREAM IS TOO HIGH
FOR THOSE WITH THEIR
EYES IN THE SKY

Adapted from the NASA film,
"With Their Eyes On The Stars"
by Mr. Aldrin

Buzz Aldrin

Jerry Della Femina

I have had dreams and
I have had nightmares.
I overcame the nightmares
because of my dreams.

Jonas Salk

Bella S. Abzug

My favorite saying is Robert Browning's, "A man's reach
should exceed his grasp, or what's a heaven for?" Except
that I would amend it in my case to " a woman's reach,
etc".

Robert Browning

Bella

Walker Percy

I know all about you: how you are neither cold nor hot. I wish you were one or the other, but since you are neither, but only lukewarm, I will spit you out of my mouth.

Revelation 3:19

Walker Percy

Anne Waldman

"Every one is one inside them, every one reminds some one of some other one who is or was or will be living."

Gertrude Stein

Anne Waldman

Hunter Thompson

"He who makes a beast of himself gets rid of the pain of being a man"

Sam Johnson

Tom Seaver

"There are but two places for an athlete to finish. First place and no place."

Tom Seaver

William F. Buckley

I know that my Redeemer liveth—

Job 19:25

Wm F Buckley

Daniel Schorr

I have always loved Edward R. Murrow's form letter to people who denounced him for his broadcasts. It was:

> 'Dear Sir or Madam:
> You may be right.'

Jim Henson

Simple is Good

Anthony Quinn & George Meany

"Do unto others as you would have them do unto you."

Herbert Gold

"There is no excellent beauty which hath not some strangeness in the proportion."

Francis Bacon

Herbert Gold

Diahann Carroll

"I need solitude like I need food and rest, and like eating and resting, solitude is most satisfying when it fits the rhythm of my needs. A regularly scheduled aloneness does not nourish me."

Hugh Prather

Diahann Carroll

Norman Cousins

"You have to go a long, long way to find the deepest and sweetest colors in the universe - unless, of course, you happen to be home."

Gustave A. Lamartine

Telly Savalas

"KNOW
THYSELF."

Socrates

Eve Merriam

"If you killed all the horses in one generation, there would be no more horses. If you killed all the poets, in the next generation, there would be just as may as ever."

John Erskine

LeRoy Neiman

THE BUSINESS MAN SAYS
"IF I DON'T DO IT FIRST SOME-
BODY ELSE WILL"

THE ARTIST SAYS
"IF I DON'T DO IT FIRST NOBODY
ELSE WILL"

LeRoy Neiman '77

Gilda Radner

PLACE
STAMP
HERE

Dear
Scott,
I've thought
and thought
and decided
on "..if you can keep
your something while
all about you... etc."
..Trumpets
from Walt Disney
Bambi
..believe it was
Bambi like
Dad say "if you
can't say
something nice,
don't say
anything
at all."

Best of luck, Gilda

Sammy Cahn

EVERYTIME YOU MAKE
THE ENDS MEET -
THEY MOVE THE ENDS!

Sammy.

Jack Dempsey

"MAKE yourself an honest man and then you may
be sure there is one rascal less in the world."

Thomas Carlyle

Jack Dempsey

Albert B. Sabin, M.D.

"If you fail to plan,
you plan to fail."

Albert B. Sabin

David Rockefeller

"I have been a banker most of my life and have never been able
to improve on the advice given many years ago by Dwight Morrow,
who said, 'Pick out the hardest subjects you can find, study
diligently, work assiduously, and give the program all the
time and effort you can muster. When you have finished, you
can then think about becoming a banker.'"

Nat Holman

"A game of ball, where players run and fall, and
never score at all, and as these questions I did ask of life,
its purpose and its task, I heard a voice within me speak:
Life's only purpose is to seek, Seeking the best in friendship."

Gerson D. Cohen

"Let your friend's dignity be as
dear to you as your own."

Talmud

James Dickey

      Struggling in vain, impatient of her load,
And lab'ring underneath the pond'rous god,
The more she strove to shake him from her breast
With more and far superior force he press'd;
Commands his entrance, and, without control,
Usurps her organs and inspires her soul.

from John Dryden's
translation of
Virgil's *Aeneid*

Arnie Levin

" Keep the whole thing going

Kimon Nikolides

Ruth Ford

"To know someone here or there
with whom you can feel there is
understanding in spite of distances
or thoughts unexpressed...that
can make of this earth a garden"

Ruth Ford

Goethe

Raymond K. Robinson

When a man loses his
enthusiasm he is bankrupt.

Herbert Ross

I believe in doing an enormous amount of preparation and
homework before I begin any project. I don't believe
in rushing around breathlessly, barking orders, screening
complaints. I don't believe much in those marvelously
intuitive inspiration moments you hear about. The
plain truth is, I'm very quiet and methodical. I walk
away from hysteria and pressure. It's taken most of my
life to learn how to do it.

Art Buchwald

Even if the meek did
inherit the earth, someone
would contest the will.

ArtB

Stephen Birmingham

"In baiting a mouse-trap with cheese,
always leave room for the mouse."

Stephen Birmingham

Jacques d'Amboise

" Stick with me Baby its champagne all the way "

Jacques d'Amboise

Henry Ford II

A quotation I would like to offer was a favorite of my grandfather, Henry Ford, the founder of Ford Motor Company and a believer in simple words and simple virtues. Carved in the wood above a fireplace at Fair Lane, his home in Dearborn, Michigan, was this saying: "Chop your own wood and it will warm you twice."

The quotation is based on a line in Henry D. Thoreau's "Walden." I've never forgotten going to my grandfather's house when I was a boy your age, or the wisdom in the words I read above the fireplace.

Marvella Bayh

"Life is not a brief candle
to me. It is a sort of
splendid torch which I have
got hold of for the moment,
and I want to make it burn
as brightly as possible
before handing it on to
future generations."

George Bernard Shaw

René Dubos

Better light a candle
than curse the darkness

Chinese Proverb

Geraldo Rivera

"We have no right to complain about any condition af-
fecting the quality of our lives, unless we are doing
something about it."

Eldon Dedini

"A journey of a thousand miles begins with The first step."

I have heard This attributed to a Turkish proverb. Also Russian.... I really can't be sure of it's origin ... probably an universal Thought.

Greetings! Eldon Dedini

Dorothy Day

"All the way to heaven is heaven, for He said, 'I am the way.'"

St. Catherine of Siena

Edmund S. Muskie

"A government has something more to do
than to govern, and levy taxes to pay the
governors. It is something more than a
police to arrest evil and punish wrong.
It must also encourage good, point out im-
provements, open roads of prosperity and
infuse life into all right enterprises.
It should combine the insight and foresight
of the best minds of the state for all the
high ends for which society is established
and to which man aspires.

   That gives us much to do."

Joshua Chamberlain

Irv Kupcinet

"As ye sow,
   so shall ye reap."

Galatians 6:7

Dotson Rader

"Life is a series of burned-out sites.
 Nobody escapes the bonfire:
 if you live -- you burn."

Andrei Voznesenski

Dotson

Rocky Graziano

"Remember, if you know how
to handle your dukes, you'll
soon realize that big guys
don't rule the world."

Robert Creeley

— coming by way
of my mother — is: "It's
always darkest before the
dawn..." Ah well... I like
the literal physical reality
it constitutes, as well as the
rest of it

Robert Creeley

Arthur Ashe

" It is what people BELIEVE that Counts, not what They THINK "

Paul Harvey

"If you don't live it, you don't believe it."

Sal Bando

I AM the WAY, the truth, AND the life

John 14:16

Suzy (Knickerbocker)

" Do what you can, with what you Have, where you are" — Suzy

Theodore Roosevelt

Buddy Young

One must know what he cannot
do in order that that he
does he does very well.

Phyllis A. Whitney

```
"I am only one,
 But still I am one.
 I cannot do everything,
 But still I can do something;
 And because I cannot do everything
 I will not refuse to do the something that I can do."
```

Edward Everett Horton

Phyllis A. Whitney

Harold Brodkey

"Ripeness is all" and "Everything is a gyp."

Shakespeare   His Father

Harold Brodkey

Oral Roberts

"Something <u>good</u> is going to happen to you!"

V. Earl Monroe, Jr.

"Opportunity at every door doth knock, but it has never been known to pick a lock". I do not know who the original author is, but it is a saying that my college coach, Clarence "Big House" Gaines repeated often, and is a favorite.

Earl

H. R. Haldeman

"Until he has been part of a cause larger than himself, no man is truly whole."

Richard Nixon

Robert Coles

"Have a heart that never hardens,
a temper that never tries,
and a touch that never hurts."

Robert Coles

Sam Levenson

Every home should set aside
a little room —
for self-improvement.

Sam Levenson

Christo

"Man is a singular creature. He has a set of gifts
which make him unique among the animals: so that,
unlike them, he is not a figure in the landscape -
he is a shaper of the landscape."

Jacob Bronowski

Michael Burke

"D'abord il faut durer."

First you have to endure.

French Proverb

Billy James Hargis

"And we know that all things work
together for good to them that love
God, to them that are the called
according to His purpose."

Stansfield Turner

By coincidence I found when I arrived at the CIA that one of my favorite quotations is engraved in the marble of the entrance to our building —

"Ye shall know the Truth and the Truth shall make you free"

John 8:32

Best wishes —

Stansfield Turner

Rear Admiral Gene R. LaRocque

"I am tired and sick of war. Its glory is all moonshine. It is only those who have neither fired a shot nor heard the shrieks and groans of the wounded who cry aloud for blood, more vengeance, more desolation. War is hell."

William Tecumseh Sherman

Cesar E. Chavez

"In a gentle way, you can shake the world."

Mahatma Gandhi

Leonard B. Boudin

"Quis custodiet ipses custodes."
Who shall guard, guards themselves.

Juvenal

Dave Brubeck

Love your enemies, bless them that curse you, do good to
them that hate you, and pray for them which despitefully
use you, and persecute you. That ye may be the children
of your Father, which in heaven: for he maketh his sun
to rise on the evil and on the good, and sendeth rain on
the just and on the unjust.

St. Matthew 5:44-45

Dave Brubeck

Howard Cosell

*"What is popular is not always
right. What is right is not
always popular."*

H Cosell

**Brendan T. Byrne &
Lee Trevino**

"The harder I work, the luckier I get."

Brendan

Denton A. Cooley, M.D.

"People say I was born under a lucky star.
But I say, the harder I work the luckier I get."

Denton A. Cooley

Jean Boudin

"Kiss the throat,
or cut it, but all."

W.D. Ruckelshaus

There are no great men in this world only great challenges which ordinary men rise to meet.

Admiral Bill Halsey

Bowie K. Kuhn

COURAGE FOR THE GREAT SORROWS OF LIFE AND PATIENCE FOR THE SMALL ONES, AND THEN WHEN YOU HAVE ACCOMPLISHED YOUR DAILY TASK, GO TO SLEEP IN PEACE. GOD IS AWAKE.

Victor Hugo

Alexander M. Haig, Jr.

"Do not let us speak of darker days; let us speak rather of sterner days. These are not dark days: these are great days -- the greatest days our country has ever lived; and we must all thank God that we have been allowed, each of us according to our stations, to play a part in making these days memorable in the history of our race."

Winston Churchill

Paul Kolton & Sylvia Porter

"An excellent plumber is infinitely more
admirable than an incompetent philosopher.
The society which scorns excellence in
plumbing because plumbing is a humble
activity and tolerates shoddiness in philosophy because it is an exalted activity
will have neither good plumbing nor good
philosophy. Neither its pipes nor its
theories will hold water."

John Gardner

A.S. Greene

"Look For A Better Way"

John W. Gardner

If you want to clear the stream,
get the hog out of the spring.

American Proverb

Karl Menninger, M.D.

It is hard for a free swimming fish to understand what is happening to a hooked one

Walter Hoving

"Without rules there can be no game, without discipline there can be no freedom, and without responsibility there can be no rights."

Walter Hoving

Vernon E. Jordan, Jr.

"We may have come over on different ships, but we're all in the same boat now."

Whitney Young

William Attwood

"To be happy with human beings, do not ask them for what they cannot give."

Tristan Bernard

Bill Attwood

Olive A. Beech

"You fool me once, shame on YOU
You fool me twice, shame on ME

Chinese Proverb

Irving S. Shapiro

"Wisdom comes seldom. It ought not
to be denied because it comes late."

Felix Frankfurter

Mildred Newman

*"He who would forget the past —
is doomed to relive it."*

George Santayana

Elinor Guggenheimer

"Grow old along with me! The best is
yet to be, the last of life, for which
the first was made. Our times are in
His hands."

Robert Browning

Elia Guggenheimer

Milton S. Eisenhower

"The essence of nostalgia is an awareness
that what has been will never be again."

Milton S. Eisenhower

John Groth

The encouraging thought
I "give" my art students
is: "In art, you don't have
to reach the top of the mountain,
where DaVinci, Rembrandt, and
Picasso dwell — if as an
artist, you make it half, or
even one quarter of the way
up, you've done darn well!"
— it is one of my own thoughts.

John Groth

Pete Seeger

"take it easy but take it"

Woody Guthrie

Pete Seeger

Pete Rozelle

```
... one of my favorite
quotations has always been
"When in doubt, punt!"
I've found it applies to
all except placekickers.
```

Pete Rozelle

Chevy Chase

"ALWAYS CARRY
A SHARP PENCIL."

Milton Friedman

"The trouble with most folks isn't so much their ignorance, as knowing so many things that ain't so".

Henry Wheeler Shaw ("Josh Billings")

Helen Reddy

"Perhaps the most valuable result of all education is the ability to make yourself do the thing you have to do, when it ought to be done, whether you like it or not. This is the first lesson to be learned."

Thomas Henry Huxley

Malcolm Forbes

"With all thy getting, get understanding."

Helen Reddy

Archibald Cox

My father had a quotation for nearly every occasion.
I suspect that the ones which I have remembered best ex-
pressed the same idea in different forms. One form was -

He started to sing
As he tackled the thing
That couldn't be done -
And he did it.

Archibald Cox

Stanley Marcus

"That which you inherit from your father
you must earn in order to possess".

Goethe

Stanley Marcus

William Sloane Coffin, Jr.

When Pope John was asked how many people worked
in the Vatican he replied, "Oh about half I guess."

How's that for a favorite saying?

B.K

Justice William O. Douglas

This arrival of the nuclear age has made me think that the most important statement we can make, and keep on making until the message is understood by every person in the universe, is this:

"The most dangerous thing a person can do these days is to be alive."

Paul R. Ehrlich

"Whatever your cause, it's a lost cause without population control".

Edmund G. Brown, Jr.

... patriotism is not so much protecting the land of our fathers as preserving the land of our children.

Jose Ortega y Gasset

Robert T. Sakowitz

"Trust all men, but cut the cards —"

Robert T. Sakowitz

Norman Lear

"You can go through life one of
two ways: wary or trusting. If you
go through life trusting you may get hurt more
often -- but you will miss none of the action.
Since action includes love, go on trusting."

Charles H. Percy

"Trust in the Lord with all thine heart and
lean not unto thine own understanding. In all thy ways
acknowledge Him and He shall direct thy paths."

Revelations 3:15

Charles H. Percy

Tom Snyder

"It's beats the
hell out of me"

Robert Klein

"Chimpanzees seldom
roller skate in the
wild"

Robert Klein

Charles Barsotti

"A BIRD IN THE HAND CAN BE
REMOVED BY A VERY SIMPLE OPERATION."
OR "TURN A FROWN UPSIDE DOWN AND ALL
THE FROWN JUICE WILL FALL OUT."
I MADE THEM UP MY OWN SELF.

Charley Barsotti

Bishop Fulton J. Sheen

It does not take much Time to make us Saints, it takes only much Love.

Fulton Sheen

Red Skelton

In life you dont give till it hurts; but until it feels good —

Red Skelton

Imogene Coca

My mother used to say, "Get off your horse and walk with the rest of the people." It's probably an old Irish saying. *Imogene Coca*

William Shatner

Have faith in the future.

[signature: William Shatner]

General Mark W. Clark

"Youth is our
most precious asset"

[signature: Mark W. Clark]

Raphael Soyer

When I was twice your age my over-eighty-year-old art teacher George W. Maynard, exhorting me to work continuously, said "You are young and have lots of time but not an ocean of time".

The older I get the more I realize the truth of his statement

Raphael Soyer.

Shari Lewis

the rights of children are worth fighting for, because children are our best known source of adults!

Shari Lewis

Howard A. Rusk, M.D.

" . . . Not to destroy but to construct
I hold the unconquerable belief
that science and peace will
triumph over ignorance and war,
that nations will come together
not to destroy but to construct,
and that the future belongs to those
who accomplish most for humanity. "

Louis Pasteur

Howard A. Rusk

Contributors to *Dear Scott*

Bella S. Abzug, New York City politician
Edwin E. "Buzz" Aldrin, Jr., former astronaut
Alta, poet
Arthur Ashe, tennis pro
Shana Alexander, columnist; television commentator
Isaac Asimov, futurist; author
William Attwood, publisher, *Newsday*
Sal Bando, third baseman, Milwaukee Brewers
Charles Barsotti, cartoonist
William M. Batten, chairman, New York Stock Exchange
Birch Bayh, United States Senator, Indiana
Marvella Bayh, wife of a United States Senator, Indiana
Olive A. Beech, chairman, Beech Aircraft Corporation
Ricky Bell, running back, Tampa Bay Buccaneers
Bernard Berkowitz, therapist; author
Angelo Bertelli, Heisman Trophy winner, Notre Dame
Stephen Birmingham, author
Julian Bond, State Senator, Georgia
Debbie Boone, popular entertainer
Victor Borge, comedian; pianist
Frank Borman, chairman, Eastern Airlines; former astronaut
Jean Boudin, poet
Leonard B. Boudin, attorney
Bill Bradley, New Jersey politician; former New York Knickerbocker
Tom Bradley, mayor of Los Angeles

Harold Brodkey, author
Heywood Hale Broun, sports commentator; writer
Edmund G. Brown, Jr., Governor, California
Helen Gurley Brown, editor, *Cosmopolitan*
Sam Brown, director, United States Volunteer Programs
Dave Brubeck, jazz musician
Bear Bryant, football coach, University of Alabama
Art Buchwald, columnist; humorist
William F. Buckley, Jr., publisher, *National Review;* columnist; television host
Michael Burke, president, Madison Square Garden
Carol Burnett, popular entertainer
Brendan T. Byrne, Governor, New Jersey
James Cagney, actor
Sammy Cahn, lyricist
Glen Campbell, popular entertainer
Milton Caniff, cartoonist
Diahann Carroll, popular entertainer
Jimmy Carter, 39th president, United States of America
Johnny Cash, popular entertainer
Chevy Chase, comedian
Cesar E. Chavez, president, United Farm Workers
John Cheever, author
Christo, artist
General Mark W. Clark, U.S.A., (ret.), president emeritus, Military College of South Carolina
Imogene Coca, comedienne
William Sloane Coffin, Jr., chaplin, The Riverside Church, New York

Gerson D. Cohen, chancellor, The Jewish Theological Seminary of America

Robert Coles, psychiatrist; author

John B. Connally, attorney; former Secretary of the Treasury, Nixon Administration

Denton A. Cooley, M.D., cardiovascular surgeon

Joan Ganz Cooney, president, Childrens' Television Workshop

Howard Cosell, television sports commentator

Margaret "Midge" Costanza, assistant to President Carter

Norman Cousins, chairman, editorial board, *Saturday Review*

Archibald Cox, attorney; special prosecutor, Nixon Administration

Harvey G. Cox, theologian, Harvard Divinity School

Robert Creeley, poet

Walter Cronkite, television newscaster

Larry Csonka, running back, New York Giants

Jacques D'Amboise, principal, New York City Ballet

Dorothy Day, founder, *The Catholic Worker*

Eldon Dedini, cartoonist

Jerry Della Femina, advertising executive

Jack Dempsey, former heavyweight boxing champion

James Dickey, poet; novelist

Phyllis Diller, comedienne

Jeane Dixon, seer

Fitzhugh Dodson, psychologist; author

William O. Douglas, Justice, United States Supreme Court

Hugh Downs, television entertainer

René Dubos, professor emeritus, Rockefeller University

Paul R. Ehrlich, biologist

Mamie Eisenhower, widow of Dwight D. Eisenhower, 34th president, United States of America

Milton S. Eisenhower, president emeritus, Johns Hopkins University

Sam J. Ervin, Jr., attorney; former United States Senator, North Carolina

Malcolm Forbes, publisher, *Forbes* magazine

Eileen Ford, director, Ford Modeling Agency

Betty Ford, wife of Gerald Ford, 38th president, United States of America

Gerald R. Ford, 38th president, United States of America

Henry Ford II, chairman, Ford Motor Company

Ruth Ford, actress

Milton Friedman, economist

G. Keith Funston, former president, New York Stock Exchange

Alan Funt, television entertainer

Zsa Zsa Gabor, actress

John W. Gardner, former chairman, Common Cause

James M. Gavin, former Lieutenant General, United States of America

Frank Gifford, television sportscaster

Herbert Gold, author

Billy Graham, evangelist

Ella Grasso, Governor, Connecticut

Rocky Graziano, former middleweight boxing champion

Dan Greenburg, author

A.S. Greene, chairman, Barber-Greene Company

John Groth, artist

George McGovern, United States Senator, South Dakota
Mary McGrory, columnist
Audrey Meadows, actress
George Meany, president, American Federation of Labor and Congress of Industrial Organizations
Karl Menninger, M.D., chairman, The Menninger Foundation
Eve Merriam, poet
Henry Miller, author
Mitch Miller, band leader
Wilbur Mills, former United States Representative, Arkansas
Liza Minelli, actress
Walter Mondale, Vice President, United States of America
V. Earl Monroe, Jr., captain, New York Knickerbockers
Mary Tyler Moore, popular entertainer
Paul Moore, Episcopal Bishop of New York
Jan Morris, author
Murray the K, disc jockey
Edmund S. Muskie, United States Senator, Maine
LeRoy Neiman, artist
Mildred Newman, therapist; author
Arnold Palmer, golf pro
Norman Vincent Peale, minister; author
Charles H. Percy, United States Senator, Illinois
Walker Percy, author
Sylvia Porter, economics journalist
Jody Powell, Press Secretary to President Carter
Anthony Quinn, actor

Dotson Rader, author
Gilda Radner, comedienne
Willis Reed, coach, New York Knickerbockers
Ronald Reagan, former Governor, California
Helen Reddy, popular entertainer
Elliot L. Richardson, United States Ambassador at Large; former Attorney General, Nixon Administration
Geraldo Rivera, television newscaster
Oral Roberts, evangelist
James Robinson, chairman, American Express
Raymond K. Robinson, editor, *Seventeen*
Sugar Ray Robinson, former middleweight boxing champion
David Rockefeller, chairman, Chase Manhattan Bank
Nelson A. Rockefeller, former Vice President, United States of America
Herbert Ross, film producer and director
Pete Rozelle, commissioner, National Football League
Dean Rusk, former Secretary of State
Howard A. Rusk, M.D., director, New York University Medical Center
W. D. Ruckelshaus, attorney; acting assistant Attorney General, Nixon Administration
Albert B. Sabin, M.D., research professor of bio-medicine, Medical University of South Carolina
Robert T. Sakowitz, chairman, Sakowitz Department Stores
Paul Samuelson, economist
Col. Harlan Sanders, founder, Kentucky Fried Chicken

Vincent Sardi, Jr., restauranteur
Telly Savalas, actor
Roy Scheider, actor
Daniel Schorr, former television newscaster; journalist
Tom Seaver, pitcher, Cincinnati Reds
Pete Seeger, folk singer
Irving S. Shapiro, chairman, E.I. DuPont de Nemours and Co., Inc.
William Shatner, actor
Bishop Fulton J. Sheen, Roman Catholic Archbishop
Eunice Kennedy Shriver, executive vice president, The Joseph P. Kennedy, Jr. Foundation
Don F. Shula, coach, Miami Dolphins
Beverly Sills, opera diva
O.J. Simpson, running back, San Francisco 49ers
Naomi Sims, model; fashion designer
Red Skelton, comedian
Cornelia Otis Skinner, actress; author
Tom Snyder, television host
Raphael Soyer, artist
Rusty Staub, outfielder, Detroit Tigers
Roger Staubach, quarterback, Dallas Cowboys
Jerry Stiller, comedian
Joan Sutherland, opera diva
Suzy (Knickerbocker), columnist
Lowell Thomas, radio commentator; author
Hunter Thompson, journalist
Sister Mary Luke Tobin, director, Church Women United
Alvin Toffler, futurist; author
John Toland, author

Lee Trevino, golf pro
Pierre Trudeau, Prime Minister, Canada
Gene Tunney, former heavyweight boxing champion
Stansfield Turner, director, Central Intelligence Agency
Harriet Van Horne, columnist
Gloria Vanderbilt, designer
Anne Waldman, poet
George C. Wallace, Governor, Alabama
Irving Wallace, author
John Wayne, actor
Lawrence Welk, orchestra leader
General William C. Westmoreland, former commanding officer, United States forces in Vietnam
Phyllis A. Whitney, author
Gene Wilder, actor
Earl Wilson, columnist
Henry Winkler, actor
Helen Yglesias, author
Andrew Young, United States Ambassador, the United Nations
Buddy Young, former halfback, Baltimore Colts
Henny Youngman, comedian
Admiral E.R. Zumwalt, Jr., retired Admiral, United States Navy